·C·O·N·T·E·N·T·S·

The rapid growth in advertising and self-service retailing during this century has itself spawned a whole new industry: that of packaging and display. Virtually everything we buy nowadays is packaged, prettified, and presented in a way that creates the desire to purchase – and paper and card are still the most widely used materials in this field.

Card engineering is where the worlds of design and engineering overlap: the card engineer, toiling away with his scalpel and his creasing rule, must wrestle with the complex structural aspects of a given brief while taking into account the design elements inherent in making the product sell. Sales kits and brochures, pop-up books and cards, cartons, display stands and point-of-sale promotional material – all of these begin life on the drawing board, when the card engineer draws up a pattern, known as a 'cutter diagram', from which he makes a cardboard mock-up, or 'blank'. The blank is sent to the client for approval, and there the artwork is laid in position. Then the blank and the artwork are sent to the factory, where a die-cutter is made up either from the blank or from the cutter drawing. The required number of items is then printed, die-cut, creased, scored or glued, and delivered in the flat to the end user.

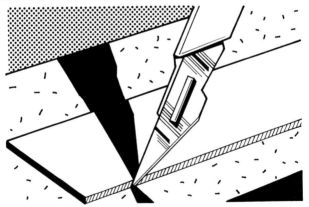

Accuracy and attention to detail are vital in card engineering, as any inaccuracies in your specifications are likely to be magnified at the die-cutting stage. If measuring, cutting, scoring and creasing are done carefully, panels should line up square and true, folds should be sharp and clean, and tucks and flaps should slide into place with just the right amount of friction. Often a millimetre or two can make all the difference between success and failure: a carton lid will not close properly, for example, if allowance has not been made for the flap which slides into the front of the carton, or if flaps are not angled back enough to prevent them buckling along a fold.

This *ON THE SPOT GUIDE* explains the basic principles of card engineering. You will learn the techniques of cutting, creasing and scoring, and how to construct mock-ups for a wide range of products, starting with simple envelopes and folders and progressing to more complex cartons, dispensers and showcards. Because accuracy is so important, the instructions given are often quite detailed, explaining why, for example, a certain dimension must be 2mm longer than another; it is advisable to read through the instructions carefully and make sure you fully understand them before tackling a project. Instructions are given below should you wish to scale up the diagrams in the book to your own dimensions, rather than drawing them up from scratch.

Scaling up using a grid

The grid system is a simple method of scaling up accurately. Make a photocopy of the diagram and draw a grid of small squares over it. Using a ruler, set square and pencil, reproduce that grid at a larger scale on a sheet of paper or board. Alternatively, lay a sheet of grid tracing paper over the original and scribe the outline of the diagram onto it. Using the tracing as a guide, transfer the diagram onto a larger scale grid. The lines and shapes within each square can be plotted by eye in the corresponding square on the larger grid.

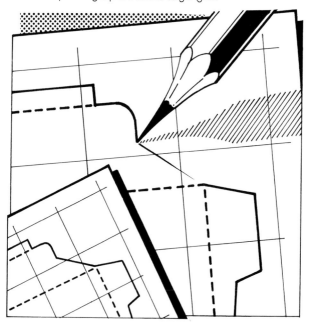

EQUIPMENT

Apart from two important items – a creasing board and creasing sticks (see pages 10-11), card engineering requires no specialist tools beyond those found in any design studio. Precision drawing instruments are essential for drawing up plans accurately.

Compasses are invaluable not only for drawing circles and arcs but also for constructing angles and dividing lines. Bow compasses offer a high degree of accuracy. A beam compass is used for drawing extra large circles and arcs.

> **❝ When using a compass for drawing circles and ellipses, avoid puncturing the surface of the paper or board with the compass point by positioning the point on a piece of card fixed in place with masking tape. ❞**

Dividers are used for measuring and for transferring dimensions. Proportional dividers are used for copying plans and diagrams on a larger or smaller scale, and for dividing lines and circles into equal parts.

Set squares are useful for quick and accurate drawing of angles. The two most common forms are the 90°-45°-45° and the 90°-60°-30°. Used with rulers or T-squares, they produce parallel lines.

T-square The top of the 'T' is fitted over the side of the drawing board; parallel lines can then be drawn by moving the T-square up and down the board.

Metal rulers are used for ruling lines, and also for guiding cutting tools along straight lines.

Scale rule This is used for enlarging or reducing diagrams to scale.

Protractor Angles can be measured to an accuracy of a quarter of a degree on a 360° protractor.

Propelling pencils When drawing up plans for folding and cutting, evenness of line is essential. Propelling pencils have a renewable point of constant weight and point size. Some are fully automatic, feeding the lead through every time the point is lifted from the paper.

Scalpels with interchangeable blades are used for fine cutting.

Craft knives are used for cutting heavy card and board.

Cutting mat This has a non-slip surface which holds the paper firmly as the knife cuts. Most have a special self-healing surface which can take repeated cutting without leaving score marks.

Adhesive Rubber-based gums dry comparatively slowly and allow time for work to be repositioned if necessary.

Double-sided tape is clean, quick and simple to use. It is useful when making up prototypes, as they often need to be taken

apart if alternations are necessary; the bond can be released by applying solvent or lighter fluid to a loosened edge. Double-sided pads are also useful.

Other equipment Apart from the above, you will also need a good pair of scissors, a stapler, a small wallpaper roller for pressing creases to make them sharp, a pair of calipers for three-dimensional measuring, a leather punch for punching small holes, and a plastic eraser for removing unwanted lines. A supply of scrap paper and tracing paper is required for drawing up plans and sketches, and a tin of lighter fuel is useful for cleaning equipment and removing greasy marks from card and paper.

CREASING

In card engineering it is important that all the folds and creases you make are crisp and accurate. But folding paper or card by hand is not precise or clean enough; the surface will 'break' along the fold, giving a ragged, untidy edge. To avoid this, the surface must be creased first, so that it folds precisely along the desired edges. In the context of card engineering, creasing means creating an embossed ridge in the surface of the card; the aim is to relieve the stress on the outer layer by compressing the fibres so that it will fold and flex easily and without breaking. To demonstrate this principle, make a crease in a sheet of card by ruling along the fold line with a ball-point pen which is out of ink. Pressing heavily with the pen creates a ridge in the surface, along which the card can be folded. The card should always be folded with the ridge or 'hinge' on the inside for minimum stretch; if the ridge is on the outside the paper is stretched taut and may rupture along the fold.

If you are taking up card engineering seriously, you will need a creasing board and creasing sticks. A creasing board consists of a block of wood with a raised metal edge, or creasing rule, down the centre. Creasing sticks are narrow blocks of very hard wood with a notch cut in one end.

Lay the card blank on the block with the fold line aligned to the metal edge. Engage the notch in the creasing stick with the metal edge and pull the stick towards you along the fold line. Apply firm pressure and make the crease with one smooth movement – try not to rub back and forth. Practise the technique on different weights of paper and card until you get a feel for it. Your local printer will make up a creasing board for you at little cost; alternatively you can make your own, using the instructions given below.

Making a creasing board

You will need a 24-in/600mm steel rule, two lengths of $1/2$in/13mm plywood (24in/600mm long x 6in/152mm wide), nails and rubber-based glue.

Cut one piece of wood in two lengthways. Glue and nail one half along one edge of the base piece. Apply a thin layer of adhesive along the exposed inner edge. Stand the steel rule vertically and glue it to this edge; the top edge of the ruler should stand proud of the upper surface of the wood by no less than 1/8in/2mm. Apply adhesive to the base and inside edge of the second piece of wood. Glue and nail in place, clamping it as tightly as possible against the steel rule. Apply G-clamps, if you have them, to ensure a tight fit.

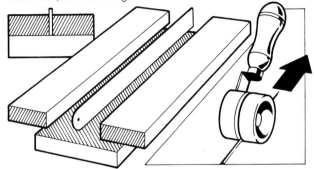

Take the sharp corners off the ruler edge by filing it with a carborundum stone or a fine file. Sand the wood smooth and apply a coat of varnish if desired.

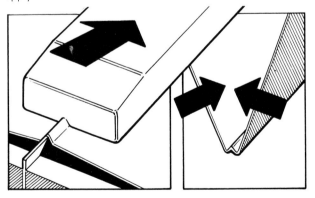

Making creasing sticks

Obtain an offcut of a very hard wood such as mahogany from a local timber merchants. Cut a piece of wood into a 'finger' 127mm long x 13mm wide x 6mm deep. Round off the top corners at one end. Using a craft knife, cut a small notch in the centre of the bottom edge. For creasing card and paper up to 400g/m² in weight, a notch approximately 1mm wide x 1mm long is suitable. Cut a bigger notch at the other end for

creasing heavier weights of card. To smooth out the notches, use the creasing stick as instructed above, working it back and forth a few times on an offcut of card.

An alternative to the creasing stick is a small wallpaper hanger's seam roller; cut a groove around the centre of the wheel and roll it along the creasing rule.

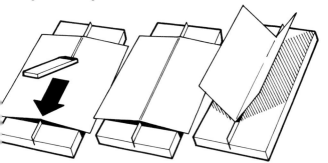

Making curved creases

Making a curved crease requires practice. The tendency is to start following the curve with the stick, whereas the correct way is to keep the stick going in a straight line while rotating the card in a clockwise direction.

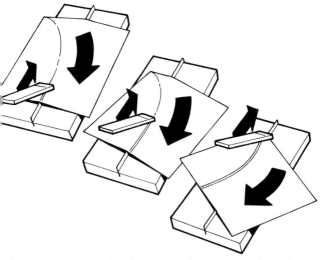

When creasing lines that do not extend to the outer edges of the paper, draw locating marks at the edges, parallel with the crease lines, to help you line them up accurately on the blade of the creasing board.

Pre-bending

Having made creases along the fold lines, the next stage is 'pre-bending'. This simply means folding along the creases in the required direction. Run your fingernail, or a wallpaper roller, along the edge of the fold to make it extra sharp.

SCORING

Heavy-weight card and board need to be scored to facilitate folding. The board is folded away from the cut of the score so that it can open out very slightly along the line of the cut. Using the point of a scalpel or craft knife, a cut is made into the surface of the board along the exact line of the fold. Apply even pressure and cut firmly, in one stroke. Knowing how deep to cut takes practice. If the cut is too shallow, the score line is ragged and doesn't flex easily; if the cut is too deep the score line will be weakened and may break with repeated handling. A correctly scored line has clean, sharp edges and will bend back easily while maintaining a degree of tension.

PERFORATING

Perforating involves making a series of very small cuts along a fold line to release tension in the paper or card and allow it to fold and flex easily. When perforating to an edge, ensure that the first and last cut don't come too close to the edge, to avoid the risk of tearing during handling.

ff When making the blanks for showcards and dispensers with front and back scores, save time by drawing all score lines on the front. Mark the ends of the back scores by piercing through the board with the tip of a scalpel, then turn the blank over and use the pierced holes as guides for the back score lines. JJ

CUTTING

A good sharp blade is essential for cutting, and is far safer than a blunt one. Keep a supply of spare scalpel and craft knife blades so that you always have a sharp blade to hand. Always work on a cutting mat and use a metal ruler as a guide (keep fingers well back from the edge to avoid accidents). Keep the blade at a constant angle and pull towards you with a swift, firm stroke. Do not try to cut through heavy card or board in one go; two or three light strokes will penetrate more easily and cleanly.

&& When cutting board, eliminate any burring along the cut edges by running a creasing stick, roller, or the flat of your fingernail along them. This gives a sharp, clean edge and protects the board from undue wear. Also use this method to achieve crisp folds and creases. 99

PAPERS AND BOARDS

The card engineer's work will stand or fall – perhaps literally – by the paper or board chosen for a given job. The right material must not only fit your design purpose but also suit the printing process you will be using (some papers stand up better than others to the pressures of printing, inking, drying, folding and cutting). Bear in mind also the purpose of the finished product: for example, a showcard intended for window display will be subjected to the rigours of sunlight and humidity, thus dictating the use of a heavier board, the cost of which must be built into the budget at the start. Finally, check that the sheet size you require can be printed and cut economically.

Weight

Generally, paper is referred to in terms of weight, and board in terms of thickness. Board thicknesses are expressed either in microns/thousandths of an inch or in sheets, the latter referring to the fact that some boards are built up from single-thickness layers.

Paper weight is measured in the imperial system in pounds per ream (500 sheets) and in the metric system in grams per square metre (g/m^2). Each grade of paper or board is available in a range of weights from light to heavy. For example, a 100 g/m^2 paper is light – about the weight of ordinary writing paper. A 225 g/m^2 paper is heavy and stiff – about the weight of the card used for menus and brochure covers.

Paper grain

Grain refers to the position of the fibres in a sheet of paper or card. The grain of paper is pronounced in machine-made papers because the mould on which they are made is a moving belt and the fibres settle in the direction of the movement of the belt.

Paper folds and creases more smoothly *with* the grain direction and roughens and cracks when folded across the grain. This is an important factor in paper and card engineering, because it can affect not only the appearance but also the strength of a finished item.

In order to find the grain direction of a sheet of paper, curl it loosely, without creasing, lengthways and then widthways.

Bounce-press gently with the flat of the hand and feel which way bends most easily.

Another way is to fold a test area of the paper swiftly in both directions with your fingertips. Folding with the grain produces a clean, crisp fold; folding against the grain produces a less satisfactory, ragged fold.

You can also identify the grain direction by tearing a test area in both directions. You will see that one torn edge is straighter and more regular than the other: this is the edge that runs along the grain.

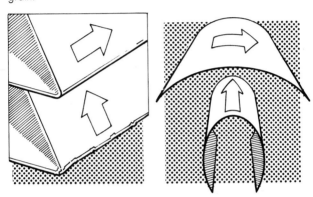

To determine the grain direction of a sheet of board, flex the sheet in your hands and then turn it through 90° and flex it the other way: it will flex more readily in the direction of the grain. Generally speaking, the grain should run parallel with the main fold on folders, booklets and cards: this helps to keep the fore-edge straight. If the grain runs crossways the edges may start to curl up eventually. With cartons and dispensers, the grain should run around the structure, perpendicular to the main scores or creases; this provides more strength across the span from one crease to another and prevents the faces from bowing inwards or outwards.

Boards for packaging and display

Generally, paper with a weight above 200g/m² is known as board. The major types used in packaging and display are:

Folding boxboards Used in the manufacture of cartons for retail packaging. Strong yet pliable, they are suitable for high-quality printing and for being cut and creased to the precision measurements demanded by high-speed mechanical packing systems. Several grades are available, including:

Solid bleached board Made entirely from bleached virgin chemical pulp and used for food packaging where purity and

clean appearance are required, eg frozen foods, cosmetics, cigarettes, pharmaceuticals, etc.

Duplex boards Composed of a back layer of unbleached chemical pulp. Used for high-grade packaging, eg food and cigarettes.

White-lined chipboard Composed of a bleached chemical pulp liner over multiple layers of waste paper. A general-purpose board used for cheaper packaging where a white printing surface is required, eg toys and electrical goods.

Corrugated board Consists of three layers of paper or board laminated together. The middle ply, or fluting, is corrugated and the outer layers, or liners, are glued to the peaks. Corrugated board is widely used in general-purpose packaging where appearance and printability are not important (though it can be white-lined for display use, for example in making support struts for large showcards and window displays). It is cheap, light yet strong, crush-resistant, and is easily folded in both directions along the vertical line of corrugation.

Display board Consists of multiple layers of recycled waste paper and board with a liner of bleached chemical pulp, subjected to pressure in the drying operation to produce a board of greater strength and rigidity than folding boxboard. Used in the manufacture of showcards, support struts, large dispensers etc.

Papers

Although board is by far the most common material used in packaging and display, it is useful to be aware of the range of papers also available. Below is a small selection.

Coated This is the term given to any paper which is given a smooth, matt or glossy surface with a coating of china clay. Particularly appropriate where a smooth even surface is needed to give a sharp image. Variations include cast coated, gloss coated, machine coated, etc.

Text Papers with interesting textures and colours, often used for booklets and brochures. Usually sized to make them suitable for printing by offset-litho.

Cover A stiff, fairly weighty paper, used for covering pamphlets and books. Has good folding, scoring and embossing qualities.

Tag A utility sheet with good folding and creasing qualities. High tear strength and stiffness permit high-speed production of smooth die-cuts. Used for folders, counter displays, greeting cards, sales kits and tags.

Kraft Made from softwood pulp, bleached or unbleached. Derives its name from the German "kraft", meaning "strength". Available in a wide range of grades and weights. The bleached papers are less strong but their whiteness enhances print quality.

TECHNICAL DRAWING

You don't need to be an expert in technical drawing to do card engineering, but the following simple procedures will make life easier and help you to achieve greater accuracy when constructing angles, lines and curves, drawing polygons and ellipses, etc.

Constructing a parallel line

1. With compass point on first line, scribe two arcs of the same radius.
2. Line up ruler against arcs and draw second line.

Bisecting a line

1. Assume line to be bisected is **AB**. Open out compasses to a radius of more than half length **AB**.
2. Scribe arcs from point **A** and point **B**.
3. Draw a line through points where arcs intersect. The vertical is exactly 90° to line **AB**.

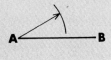

Erecting a perpendicular from a fixed point

1. Scribe two arcs of equal radius to produce points **A** and **B**.
2. Open out compasses to a larger radius and scribe arcs from **A** and **B**.
3. Draw a line through point where arcs intersect to produce a perpendicular.

Erecting a perpendicular from a point to a line

1. From a given point, scribe two arcs of equal radius to cross line, producing points **A** and **B**.
2. Follow procedure for bisecting a line (see above).
3. Draw a perpendicular connecting point to line.

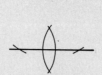

Dividing a line into equal parts

This is an accurate method for dividing a line without measuring with a ruler, which can cause inaccuracies if the total measurement is not easily divided arithmetically.

 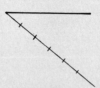

1. Assume line **AB** is to be divided into five equal parts. Drop a line from **A**, at any angle or length.
2. Set compasses to a small radius and mark off required number of divisions, in this case five.
3. Draw a line joining final mark on angled line to **B**. Work back from each mark, using ruler and set square to draw lines parallel to first line drawn (see below). Where these lines cross line **AB**, they mark equal divisions.

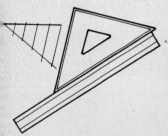

Drawing parallel lines
Line up a set square to first line and butt up a ruler to it. Holding ruler steady, move set square along ruler to next position and draw parallel line. Repeat to end.

Bisecting an angle
1. From **A**, scribe an arc that crosses both lines.
2. Open compasses out to a larger radius (the wider the angle the larger the radius). Scribe arcs from points **B** and **C**.
3. Draw a line from **A** through point where arcs intersect.

 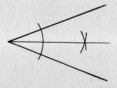

Constructing angles

Drawing angles accurately is an essential part of paper and card engineering. While a set square and protractor are invaluable tools, inaccuracies can occur if they move while you are drawing, or when they become worn through use. Constructing angles geometrically guarantees accuracy every time. Below are the angles most commonly used.

60° angle

1. From **A** scribe an arc to create point **B**.
2. Keeping the same radius, scribe an arc from **B** to cross first arc.
3. Draw a line from **A** through intersection of arcs.

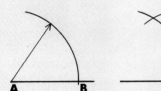

30° angle

1. Construct an angle of 60°, as above.
2. Bisect angle (see page 17).

 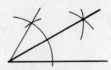

90° angle

1. Mark off an angle of 60°. Keeping the same compass radius, mark off 60° again from **A** to create a 120° angle.
2. Scribe intersecting arcs from **A** and **B** (ie, bisect angle formed by dotted lines on diagram).
3. Draw a vertical through points where arcs intersect.

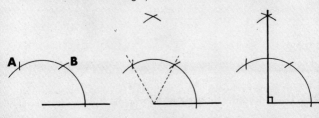

45° angle
1. Construct an angle of 90°.
2. Bisect angle as before.

CONSTRUCTING TRIANGLES
There are various triangular forms, but the two you are most likely to use in card engineering are the equilateral, in which all the sides (and all the angles) are equal, and the isosceles, in which two sides (and two angles) are equal.

Equilateral triangle
1. Open compasses to radius **AB** and scribe arcs from **A** and then **B** to intersect at **C**.
2. Triangle **ABC** is equilateral.

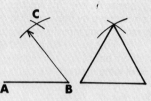

Isosceles triangle
1. Open compasses to a radius equal to required height of triangle and scribe arcs from **A** and **B** to intersect at **C**.
2. Draw lines **AC** and **BC** to form isosceles triangle.

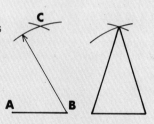

Blending lines and curves
Many card constructions, such as folders and cartons, include corners that are curved, or 'filleted'. Curved corners not only improve the appearance of an object, they are also stronger and less prone to wear and tear than square corners.
Blending a curve into a straight edge is not difficult. The trick is to find the centre of the curve: if this is pin-pointed accurately, the ends of the curve will blend exactly with the straight edges.

Curving a right-angled corner
1. Open compasses to required radius. With centre **A**, scribe arcs to cut the lines of the angle at **B** and **C**. With the same radius, scribe arcs from **B** and **C** to intersect at **O**. This marks the centre of the curve.
2. Keeping the same radius, and with centre **O**, scribe an arc to form the curved corner.

Curving an angled corner

1. Open compasses to required radius and construct lines parallel with the lines of the angle, to intersect at **O**. This marks the centre of the curve.
2. With the same radius, and centre **O**, scribe an arc to form the curved corner.

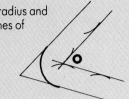

CONSTRUCTING POLYGONS

A polygon is a figure with three or more sides. Such constructions are often incorporated into the design of gift packs, cartons and presentation and display items since they are eye-catching and more unusual than squares and circles. Examples of polygons include the pentagon (five sides), hexagon (six sides), heptagon (seven sides), octagon (eight sides), nonagon (nine sides) and decadon (ten sides).

Drawing a square

This method ensures that all four corners of the square are exactly 90°.
1. Draw the side **AB**. From **A** erect a perpendicular and mark off the length of side **AC**.
2. With centres **B** and **C** draw arcs, radius equal to length of side of square, to intersect at **D**. Draw lines **CD** and **BD** to complete square.

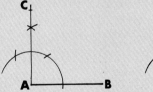
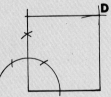

Constructing a hexagon

It is possible to construct a hexagon within a given circle, as follows:

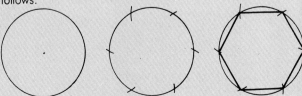

1. Draw a circle, radius equal to length of side of hexagon.
2. From any point on the circumference, step the radius around the circle six times.
3. Connect the six points to form a hexagon.

To construct any given polygon

Using this method, it is possible to construct a polygon with any number of sides.

1. Draw a line **AB** equal in length to one of the sides, and bisect it.

2. Extend perpendicular. From **A** construct an angle of 45° to intersect bisector at point **4**. Point **4** is the centre of a circle containing a square. From **B** construct an angle of 60° to intersect bisector at point **6**. Point **6** is the centre of a circle containing a hexagon.

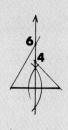

3. Bisect the distance between **4** and **6** to obtain centre for pentagon (five sides). With centre at **5**, scribe a circle, radius **5** to **A**.

4. Step the radius **AB** around the circle five times. Connect the five points to form the pentagon.

5. Measure distance between points **5** and **6** and mark off above point **6**. This is the centre of a circle containing a heptagon (seven sides); the radius will be **7** to **A**. By marking off points on the perpendicular in this way, the centres of circles containing any polygon can be obtained.

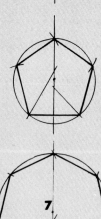

Finding the centre of a circle or arc
1. Draw any two chords (ie straight lines crossing the circle, as shown). These can be of any length.
2. Construct perpendiculars to bisect the chords. Where the perpendiculars intersect is the centre of the circle.

Drawing ellipses
A circle that is viewed at an angle, rather than square on, is foreshortened and becomes an ellipse.

There are two main axes on an ellipse. The major axis is the longest measurement, equal to the diameter of the circle that the ellipse is derived from. The minor axis is at right-angles to the major axis and is the shortest measurement on the ellipse. The greater the angle of tilt, the more foreshortening on the minor axis and the narrower the ellipse appears. The major axis stays the same whatever the degree of tilt.

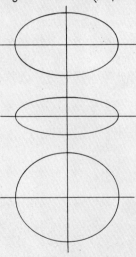

There are two main methods for constructing an accurate ellipse. The most commonly known method involves using a trammel as a drawing guide. Another way is by constructing the ellipse by concentric circles. Both methods are described below.

Constructing an ellipse by concentric circles

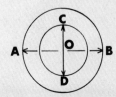

1. Determine the required size and angle of the ellipse and draw the major axis **AB** and the minor axis **CD** accordingly, making

sure that they are at right-angles to each other. With centre **O** and radius **OA**, scribe the outer circle. With centre **O** and radius **OD**, scribe the inner circle.

2. Extend line **CD** to outer circle. Divide the circle into an equal number of parts. Here the sectors are divided at 60° and 30°, but you can make as many divisions as you like and at any angle. The more divisions the more accurate the ellipse will be.
3. Where each line crosses the inner circle, draw a horizontal, and where the line crosses the outer circle, draw a vertical to meet the horizontal.
4. Either by hand or using French curves, join up the intersections to form the ellipse.

Drawing an ellipse using a trammel
To make a trammel, simply cut a strip of paper or card at least half the length of the major axis of the circle and with one straight edge.

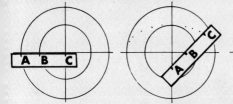 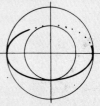

1. Follow the instructions in step 1 above for drawing up the inner and outer circles. Hold the trammel against either axis so that one end overlaps the spot where the major and minor axis meet. On the trammel, mark off the centre spot **C** and the spots where the circles cross, **B** and **C**.
2. Lay the trammel so that mark **A** touches the minor axis and mark **B** touches the major axis (you can start anywhere). Make a light dot at mark **C**. Move the trammel slightly to the left or right, making sure that you keep **A** on the minor axis and **B** on the major axis. Make another light dot at mark **C**. Continue around the circle plotting a series of dots, until you have described a complete ellipse. The more dots plotted, the greater the accuracy of the finished ellipse.
3. Join up the dots to form the ellipse.

chapter one

ENVELOPES AND FOLDERS

Practise your cutting,
folding and measuring
skills on these relatively
simple constructions

With direct mail increasing in popularity as a promotional medium, envelopes and folders now play more than merely a functional role in carrying and protecting their contents: they are an integral part of the package. It is important to choose the right material for the job: the look and feel of a particular paper or board can strongly enhance the finished design, but there are other factors to consider, including strength, bulk, postal weight and printability.

Envelopes

There is a wide range of envelope styles, which fit into two broad categories:

1. Wallet or pocket envelopes, with flaps on the shorter side. Used for mailing booklets, magazines, catalogues, reports, etc. Wide seams and flaps ensure maximum protection during transit. Expansion envelopes are used for bulky correspondence and for package and rack sales. Closure variations include gummed, self-sealing, tuck-in, string-and-button and metal clasp.

2. Banker envelopes have flaps on the long side. Used for all types of correspondence, greeting cards, invitations, etc. Various styles and sizes available. Depending on the specific use in mind, you can choose from a wide range of bond, cartridge, manilla and vellum papers, as well as duplex or folding box board for larger envelopes.

Folders

Folders are widely used in marketing, in the form of pre-packs and sales presenters. Their function is to contain and protect their contents while forming an attractive package which enhances the client's corporate image. This section presents some commonly used folder constructions, each of which can be modified to the requirements of a particular design brief. Folding boxboard of around ·020 inch/500 microns is suitable for most folders. Speciality boards and papers are also appropriate, including embossed, laminated and marbled surfaces.

DOCUMENT FOLDER

This is a simple one-piece folder with a pocket formed from a single flap glued down one edge.

Example illustrated measures 8¼in/209mm x 5¾in/146mm when closed.

*See inside front and rear cover for key

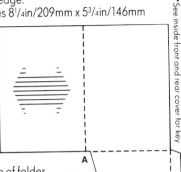

1. Determine size and shape of folder. Draw up plan of folder as in diagram, ensuring that the paper grain runs parallel to the centre crease. Add an extra 5mm to dimensions all round, to aid insertion of papers into folder. Note that inside edge **A** of bottom flap starts 3mm in from centre crease of folder and is angled back so as to be clear of centre crease when folder is closed.

Cut out folder and crease along all dotted lines, using a creasing board. Pre-bend creases.

2. Apply glue or double-sided tape along underside of glue flap and fold inwards. Remove backing strip from tape and fold pocket flap up. Apply pressure along glue area to fix in place.

'WITH-CAPACITY' DOCUMENT FOLDER

This is a one-piece 'with-capacity' folder, having a centre spine and a shaped pocket with box edges which allow a greater quantity of material to be held.

Example illustrated measures 8¼in/210mm x 6in/152mm x ¼in/6mm.

1. Determine required dimensions of folder and draw up plan as in diagram. Grain of card should run parallel to centre crease. The pocket can be any shape, height and depth you like: determine the depth based on the number of sheets to be held and draw double creases on pocket accordingly. Double crease forming centre spine of folder is 1mm wider than creases on pocket, to allow for front cover being folded over pocket. Note that inside edge **A** of bottom flap starts 2mm in from centre

crease of folder so as to be clear of centre crease when folder is closed.

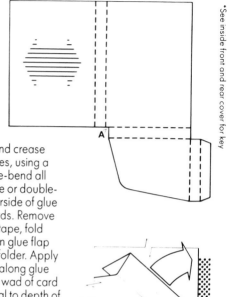

*See inside front and rear cover for key

2. Cut out folder and crease along all dotted lines, using a creasing board. Pre-bend all creases. Apply glue or double-sided tape to underside of glue flap and fold inwards. Remove backing strip from tape, fold pocket up and align glue flap with back edge of folder. Apply only light pressure along glue area. Make a thick wad of card or other stiff material to depth of pocket. Insert this into corner of pocket, as shown, and apply firm pressure along glue area to secure. This method ensures that the glue flap can be firmly adhered, without crushing the front of the pocket in the process.

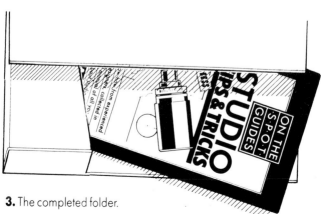

3. The completed folder.

DOCUMENT FOLDER

A one-piece, non-glued document folder with slot-fastened corner pocket, designed to hold a small quantity of paper. This is known in the trade as a 'non-capacity' folder, as it folds flat and does not have expandable or box edges.

When designing a flat folder, make it about 1/4in/6mm larger all round than the papers it is designed to hold: this enables the papers to be slipped into the folder more easily.

Example illustrated measures 8in/203mm x 5³/4in/146mm.

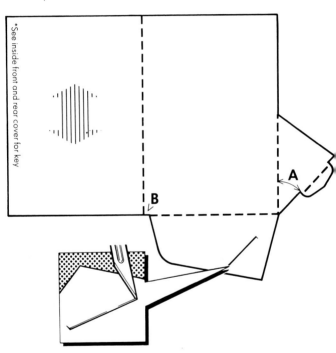

*See inside front and rear cover for key

1. Draw up plan of folder to dimensions required, following the diagram. Card grain runs parallel to centre crease.

● It is important that angle marked **A** on side flap is exactly 45°.
● Locking tongue on side flap is not centred on the edge, but positioned near the top. Note also that crease along tongue is positioned about 3mm forward of edge of side flap. This helps to stop the tongue coming out.
● Inside edge **B** of bottom flap starts 2mm in from centre crease of folder. This allows for clearance when folding front cover of folder over.

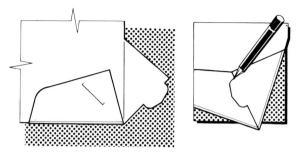

2. Cut out folder and crease along all dotted lines. Pre-bend all creases. To establish length and position of slot in lower flap, fold up lower flap, then fold side flap over it. Hold side flap in place with one hand while making light pencil dots on lower flap at each corner of tongue on side flap. Open out both flaps again. Turn folder over and make a straight cut between the pencil dots. Make right-angle cuts at each end of the slot, approximately 3mm long, in direction of left-hand corner. These cuts allow tongue to slide into slot more easily.

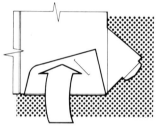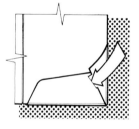

3. Turn folder over again and make up pocket by folding side flap over bottom flap and sliding tongue into slot.

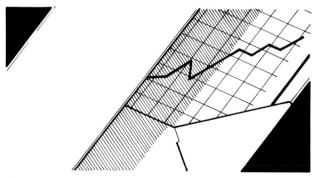

4. Bring front of folder over to complete.

WALLET-TYPE FOLDER

This is a simple wallet-type 'with-capacity' folder with
expandable pocket, suitable for holding documents, artwork,
publicity material, etc.
Example illustrated measures 8in/203mm x 6in/152mm.

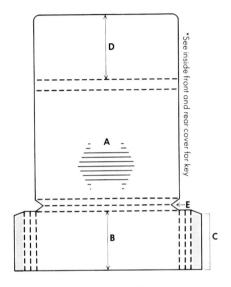

*See inside front and rear cover for key

1. Determine required size and shape of folder, bearing in mind
that it should be approximately 3mm bigger all round than the
maximum size of the papers to be held, to allow for ease of
insertion. Determine maximum capacity required of folder — i.e.
the maximum number of sheets it is to hold. This will determine
width of triple creases forming sides and base of pocket and
double crease forming spine along top of folder.
Draw up plan of folder as in diagram, starting with a rectangle
A for back of folder. Ensure that card grain runs widthways.
Determine required depth of pocket **B**: as a guide, it is normally
about half the depth of the back of the folder. Determine
required width of triple creases forming sides and base of
pocket. Glue flaps **C** should be not less than 19mm wide,
depending on size of folder. Top flap **D** should be deep enough
to overlap pocket when closed. Double crease between **A** and
D is the same width as triple creases at sides and base of
pocket.
Cut out folder and crease along all dotted lines,using a creasing
board. Cut out 'V'-shaped indents at points marked **E**, cutting in
from edge to a depth of no less than half width of triple crease.
Ensure that point of 'V' lies exactly on centre crease.

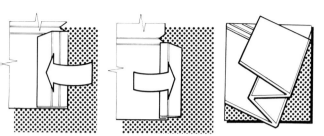

2. Form concertina folds of pocket sides as follows: 1 Fold in flaps and pre-bend crease on outside edge. 2 Now fold flap back on itself on centre crease. 3 Fold glue flap inwards again and pre-bend third crease.

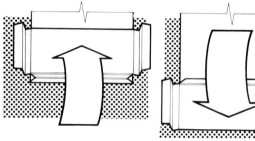

3. Concertina-fold bottom of pocket in same way as sides: 1 Fold up pocket and pre-bend crease along bottom edge. 2 Fold pocket back on itself along centre crease. 3 Fold up again and pre-bend third crease.

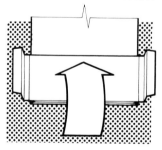

4. Apply glue or double-sided tape to underside of glue flaps. Peel backing strips from tape. Fold up pocket, ensuring that glue flaps are positioned in front of the creases at bottom of pocket, not behind. Apply pressure along glue areas to secure.

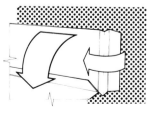

5. Pre-bend double crease running between back of folder and top flap. Fold flap over to close. Flap can either be left loose or tucked inside pocket.

DISPLAY FOLDER

This is a useful folder for storing and displaying brochures and other printed literature. Cut from a single piece of card, with no gluings, the folder has two rigid inside pockets with cut-out display 'windows' and closes to form a wallet with slot-in tab fastening.

Example illustrated measures 3³/₄in/95mm x 7in/178mm x ¹/₂in/13mm.

1. Measure up dimensions of papers to be held in pockets of folder and determine how many sheets each pocket is to hold. Draw up plan of folder as in diagram, based on these measurements. Card grain runs widthways.

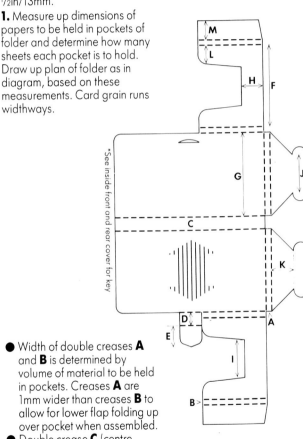

*See inside front and rear cover for key

● Width of double creases **A** and **B** is determined by volume of material to be held in pockets. Creases **A** are 1mm wider than creases **B** to allow for lower flap folding up over pocket when assembled.

● Double crease **C** (centre spine of folder) should be twice the width of double crease **A**, plus 1mm.

● Position of locking flap and slot will determine maximum height of inside pockets. Locking flap should measure at least 25mm wide, depending on size of folder, and is centred on the left-hand edge of folder. Dimension **D** on locking flap is

equal to width of centre spine **C**, plus 1mm. Dimension **E** on locking flap should be long enough so that flap protrudes at least 13mm into slot on right-hand side of folder when closed.
- Slot for locking tab should be exactly the same width as locking tab and positioned directly opposite it. Straight edge of slot should be at least 13mm in from edge.
- Dimension **F** on pockets should equal dimension **G** on front and back of folder.
- Dimension **H** on pockets should be not less than 25mm, depending on size of folder.
- As a guide, width **I** should be approximately half overall width of pocket, and centred.
- Width **J** on bottom flaps is equal to width **I** on pocket 'window'.
- Dimension **K** is equal to dimension **H**.
- Width **L** on side pockets is equal to width **M**, ie narrowest part of pocket front, not widest part, so that flap **M** doesn't show when pocket is assembled.

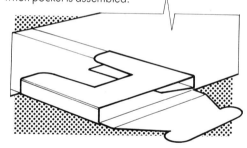

2. Having checked all the dimensions, cut out folder and crease along all dotted lines, Using a scalpel, cut out slot for locking tab. To assemble folder, pre-bend all creases. Fold in pockets as shown.

3. Fold bottom flaps up over pockets and lock in place by inserting curved ends of locking flaps behind.

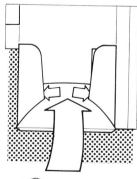

4. Close wallet and lock by inserting tab through slot.

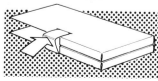

CONCERTINA BOOKLET

A simple but ingenious design for a concertina booklet with its own integral case. The whole thing is made from one piece of card, and without any gluings. This type of booklet is a neat and convenient way of storing or displaying information such as charts, maps, diagrams or photographs, or could make an eye-catching mailing shot.

Example illustrated measures 5in/127mm x 3in/76mm when closed.

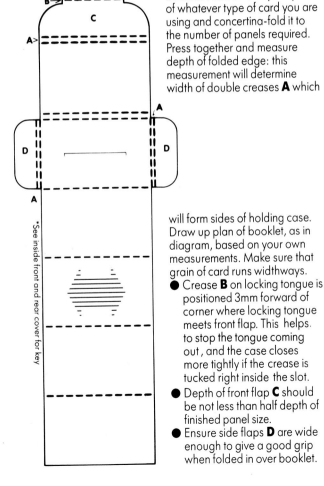

1. Determine size, shape and number of panels required for booklet. Next take a spare piece of whatever type of card you are using and concertina-fold it to the number of panels required. Press together and measure depth of folded edge: this measurement will determine width of double creases **A** which will form sides of holding case. Draw up plan of booklet, as in diagram, based on your own measurements. Make sure that grain of card runs widthways.

● Crease **B** on locking tongue is positioned 3mm forward of corner where locking tongue meets front flap. This helps to stop the tongue coming out, and the case closes more tightly if the crease is tucked right inside the slot.

● Depth of front flap **C** should be not less than half depth of finished panel size.

● Ensure side flaps **D** are wide enough to give a good grip when folded in over booklet.

*See inside front and rear cover for key

In this example, they are 25mm wide, excluding width of double fold. Cut out booklet and crease along all dotted lines, using a creasing board.

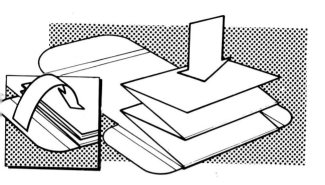

2. To make up booklet, pre-bend all creases and fold panels concertina-style, as shown.
3. Fold side flaps in over folded panels.
4. To establish length and position of locking slot in front panel, fold front flap over as shown.
5. Hold front flap firmly in place and mark inside corners of locking tab with light pencil dots.
6. Open booklet out fully and turn over. With locking tab facing you, use a scalpel to cut a straight line between the pencil dots. Then cut small right-angle slits, about 3mm long, at each end, facing away from you.

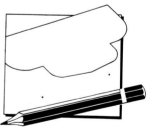

7. Make up booklet again. Fold front flap over and slide locking tab into slot to close.

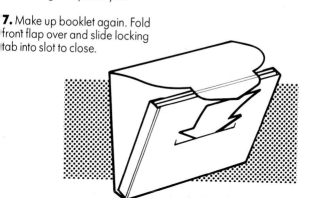

SLOT-FASTENED ENVELOPE

A simple, one-piece, non-glued envelope with slot fastening, designed to carry letters, invitation cards, etc.
Example illustrated measures 6½in/165mm x 4in/101mm.

1. Determine required size and shape of envelope. Draw a few sketches to help visualize how you want the finished envelope to look. The example illustrated here is a rectangular envelope with a narrow base flap and a deep top flap, but the proportions can be altered to suit your own requirements. For example, you may want a deeper envelope, or a longer, narrower one; or you may prefer a deep base flap and a narrower top flap.

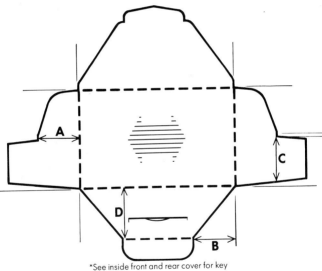

*See inside front and rear cover for key

2. Draw up plan of envelope. First draw a rectangle to the size and proportions required, making sure the corners are absolutely square. Work out depth of top and bottom flaps and width of side flaps and draw them up as in diagram.

● It is important that dimensions marked **A** on side flaps are equal to dimensions **B** so that when bottom flap is folded up over side flaps (see step 4) the corners tuck in neatly.
● Dimensions **C** on side flaps should be 2mm shorter than dimensions **D** on bottom flap to allow for clearance when folding bottom flap over side flaps.

● Draw shoulders and bottom edges of side flaps at a slight angle, as shown, so that when folded in, the side flaps are clear of the crease along the top and bottom of the envelope. Having checked that all the dimensions are correct, cut out envelope. Crease along all dotted lines using creasing board. Pre-bend all creases.

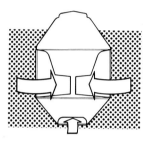 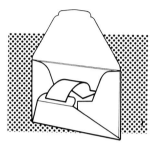

3. Fold in side flaps.
4. Raise up lower flap, tucking tongue behind side flaps to lock in place.

5. To establish width and position of slot in lower flap, fold down top flap and mark inner corners of locking tongue with light pencil dots. Now open envelope out again and turn over, with locking flap facing you. Using a scalpel, cut a straight line between the pencil dots. Cut a small 'thumbnail' indent centred on edge nearest tongue. Make 3mm right-angle cuts at each end of slot, in direction of locking flap. The thumbnail indent and cuts allow the tongue to be easily inserted into the slot when closing the envelope.

6. To close envelope, bend top flap slightly and slide tongue into slot.

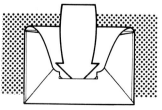

'WITH-CAPACITY' ENVELOPE

This envelope is broadly similar to the one on page 36, but with the addition of box sides designed to hold a greater quantity of material. The side flaps lock together in the centre to hold the envelope rigid and give added strength. This is known in the trade as a 'with-capacity' envelope.

Example illustrated measures 6½in/165mm x 4in/101mm x ½in/13mm.

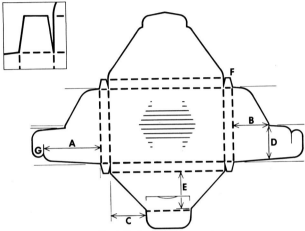

*See inside front and rear cover for key

1. Determine required size and format of envelope, then draw up a plan as shown. Start with inner rectangle forming front of envelope. Determine required depth of envelope (based on thickness of material to be held) and draw double creases forming box sides. Then draw side flaps.

● Side flaps should be wide enough so that locking tabs overlap at centre when side flaps are folded inwards. To ensure this, dimensions **A** on side flaps must be equal to half width of inner rectangle.

● Dimensions **B** on side flaps are equal to dimensions **C** so that when bottom flap is folded up over side flaps the corners tuck in neatly.

● Dimensions **D** on side flaps should be 2mm shorter than dimensions **E** on bottom flap to allow for clearance when folding bottom flap up over side flaps (see step 4).

● Draw shoulders and bottom edges of side flaps at a slight angle, as shown, so that when folded in, side flaps are clear of creases along top and bottom of envelope.

Having checked that all dimensions are correct, cut out envelope. Using a creasing board, crease along all dotted lines shown on diagram and pre-bend all creases. At each of the four corners marked **F** make angled cuts from crease lines to create tabs that fold in neatly when envelope is closed. Make incisions half depth of dimension **D** into locking tabs at points marked **G**.

2. Fold in corner flaps **F**.

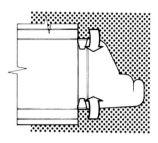

3. Fold side flaps inwards and lock by hooking together the locking tabs, as shown.

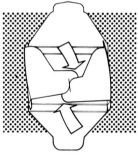

4. Raise up lower flap, tucking tongue behind side flaps to lock in place. To establish length and position of slot in lower flap, follow instructions given on page 37, step **5**.

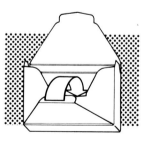

5. To close envelope, bend top flap slightly and slide tongue into slot.

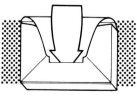

HEXAGONAL ENVELOPE

With the aid of a compass, ruler and set square, you can make unusual envelopes and gift packs that offer a refreshing change from the normal square or rectangular designs. This hexagonal envelope with overlapping flaps is made from one piece of card, with no gluings. The flaps must be drawn and cut carefully so that they meet exactly in the centre when closed.
Example illustrated measures 5in/127mm in diameter.

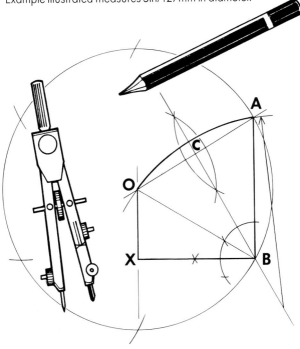

1. Determine size of envelope required and draw a hexagon to that size (see page 20). Establish shape of six outer flaps as follows: draw a line **AO** from one point of hexagon to centre. From next point down, draw line **BX** at 90° to line **AB**. Now draw line **OX** at 90° to line **BX**.
If line **AO** is curved slightly, rather than straight, the finished appearance of the envelope is more pleasing. To draw the curve, find centre of line **AO** and draw a light pencil line **CB**. With a pair of compasses, place pencil point at **A** and compass point anywhere on line **CB**. Judge by eye how much of a curve this will give you, adjusting the position of the compass point if necessary until you get the right degree of curve.

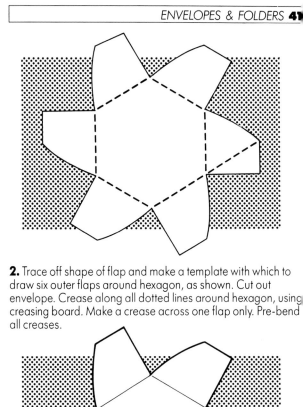

2. Trace off shape of flap and make a template with which to draw six outer flaps around hexagon, as shown. Cut out envelope. Crease along all dotted lines around hexagon, using creasing board. Make a crease across one flap only. Pre-bend all creases.

3. Make up envelope by folding in first flap to left of creased flap and continuing round in sequence.

4. To close envelope, raise last flap, bend at crease and tuck in as shown.

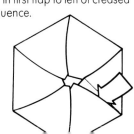

chapter two

POP-UPS

This section demonstrates three simple pop-up techniques which can be used as starting points for imaginative three-dimensional greeting card ideas

Since their invention in 1855, pop-up books and greeting cards have continued to amuse and amaze adults and children alike. The range of ingenious ideas to be found in children's pop-up books is beyond the scope of this book, but three pop-up mechanisms — the connecting bar, hinge and V-fold — are explained in this section because they are simple and you can use them to design personalized greeting cards to send to family and friends. Each is the starting point for a wide range of ideas: the images which pop-up or move in surprising ways are activated simply by opening or closing the card. The imaginative possibilities come from your choice of design, mechanism and message, all working in harmony.

Before starting, it is advisable to work out your pop-up shapes on rough paper first, to make sure they won't protrude beyond the edges of the card when it is closed. Use thin card or thick paper, and make sure the grain runs parallel with the main fold.

CONNECTING BAR MECHANISM

The effect of this mechanism is to create a multi-layered design from a single piece of card, with no gluings. When the card is opened out to an angle of 90°, giving a horizontal and a vertical plane, the overlapping layers inside are pulled upright by means of small connecting bars to create a three-dimensional image.

Example illustrated measures 6in/152mm x 4½in/114mm when closed.

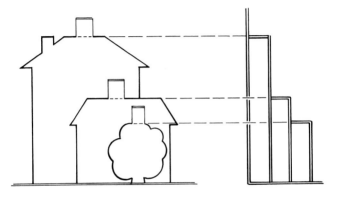

1. First determine size and format of card. Draw the overlapping planes of the cut-out design to size on a piece of paper and determine the distance between each plane.

- The distance between planes can be varied, but the maximum distance should be 20mm, otherwise the connecting bars become too long and obtrusive.
- When designing the cut-out shapes, remember to incorporate a straight horizontal line 10mm long into the top edge of each plane, as in the tree in this example: this forms the front edge of the connecting bar. Position the connecting bar so that it links up with the plane behind.
- The distance between the top edge of the card and the top edge of the back plane must be at least twice the depth of the connecting bar on the back plane, otherwise the top of the back plane will protrude from the card when it is closed.
- The cut-out shapes should be positioned no less than 20mm from the outer edges of the card, particularly near the centre fold. This will lessen the risk of tearing during repeated handling.

2. Because the pop-up shapes are cut out of the card itself, you will need an extra two pages to wrap around the outside of the card to cover up the holes created. On your sheet of card, draw up plan of pop-up card, with four pages of equal size. Grain of card should run parallel to main fold. From your sketch, trace off outline of back plane, remembering to include connecting bar. Measure length of connecting bar and draw a line this distance below centre crease. This gives you correct position of base line of back plane. Trace outline of back plane in position on card. Draw base line for centre plane at correct distance (ie length of connecting bar) from base line of back plane. Trace outline of centre plane in position. Repeat for front plane.

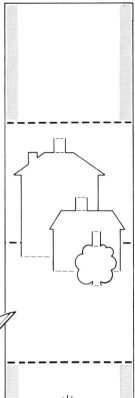

*See inside front and rear cover for key

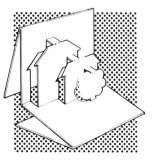

3. Cut out along all cut lines and crease and perforate where indicated. Pre-bend all creases and perforations (the connecting bars are easier to bend if the back edges are perforated rather than creased). Fold top and bottom pages to back of card and stick down at outer edges only.

*See inside front and rear cover for key

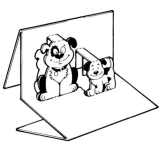

This design uses a variation on the connecting bar mechanism shown on p45. Here, the dog and pup are not overlapping; both connecting tabs are cut from the back of the card itself.

HINGED MECHANISM

This mechanism is simple to make and gives a lot of movement. The pop-up piece is glued to a hinged section which is constructed so that, as the card is opened, it causes the pop-up to swing up in the air. The element of surprise, and the potential for amusing designs, make this a popular choice of mechanism. So that the pop-up piece remains hidden when the card is closed, it is important to calculate its size and shape in relation to the card, and also its position on the centre crease. When designing the pop-up piece, include one short, straight edge on the left side: this is the point that will be glued to the hinged mechanism.

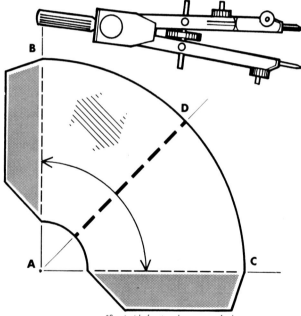

*See inside front and rear cover for key

1. Draw up and cut out the pop-up shape. To make the hinged mechanism, draw an angle of 90° and bisect it to produce lines **AB**, **AC**, **AD**. These lines are equal in length to connecting edge of pop-up shape, plus an extra 10mm. Set compasses to radius of 10mm. With centre **A**, scribe an arc to cut all three lines. Keeping centre **A**, set compasses to radius **AB** and scribe an arc through **BDC**. Add on the glue flaps, which are angled back at the top and straight across the bottom. Cut out and crease along dotted lines.

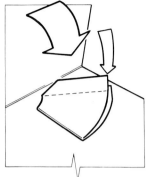

2. Cut out card to desired dimensions and make centre crease. Apply double-sided tape to underside of glue flaps on hinged mechanism but do not remove backing strips. Fold glue flaps under and lay mechanism in position, lining up centre crease with centre crease of card. Remove backing strip from right glue flap only and glue in position. Bring left side of mechanism over to fold in half.

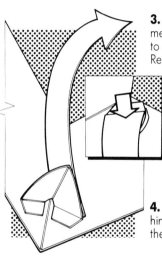

3. Glue pop-up shape to mechanism with edge butting up to glue flap as indicated. Remove backing strip from glue flap and bring front of card over to close. Apply pressure to glue area.

4. When the card is opened the hinged mechanism unfolds and the pop-up piece swings upwards.

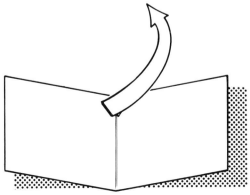

*See inside fr

V-FOLD MECHANISM

This mechanism is one of the simplest to construct and is adaptable in many different ways. The pop-up shapes are attached to the card by means of flaps which can be arranged either in a V-shape or an inverted V-shape, depending on the effect you wish to create. As with the connecting bar mechanism on page 45, realistic 3-D scenes can be made up from several planes. The advantage of the V-fold is that there are no holes or connecting bars visible, but it cannot be cut from a single sheet of card, and there are several gluings – which would make the card more expensive to produce commercially.

1. Cut out card to required dimensions and crease down centre. On rough paper, sketch a layout of the opened card with the pop-up shapes in position. The angles either side of the centre crease must be equal and should be neither too steep nor too shallow: between 20° and 50° is recommended.

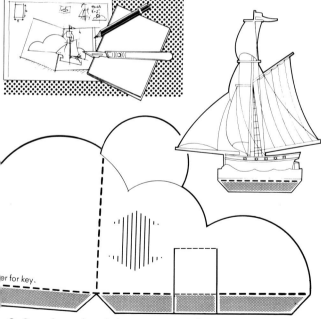

er for key.

2. On a sheet of card, draw up pop-up shapes. Note that the base crease lines are angled down slightly from the centre line – about 2° from the horizontal. This helps the shapes to stand up straight: if the base line is not angled, the shapes appear, through an optical illusion, to be leaning forward. The corners of the glue flaps are angled at 45°.

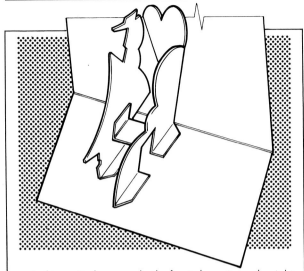

In this particular example, the front plane sits on the right-hand page only, so it must be attached to the back plane with a connecting bar, which pulls the front plane up as the card is opened. Depth of connecting bar is equal to distance between front and back planes.

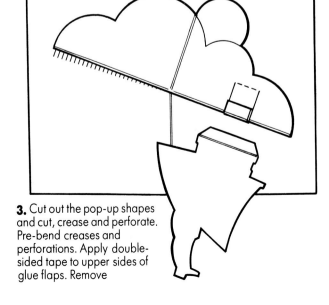

3. Cut out the pop-up shapes and cut, crease and perforate. Pre-bend creases and perforations. Apply double-sided tape to upper sides of glue flaps. Remove

backing strip from right-hand glue flaps only and fold all glue flaps to back (except for flap on connecting bar). Glue back plane in position on right-hand side of card, then fold back flat and apply pressure along glue flap. Glue front plane in position then fold back and glue to connecting bar on centre plane.

Detail shows side view of connecting bar in operation.

4. Fold back plane over from centre crease until flat. Remove backing strip from glue flap. Lightly hold shapes down and fold front of card over. Press firmly along glue area. Working in this way guarantees that the angles left and right of the centre fold are exactly equal; if you had glued down the shapes on both sides of the centre crease before closing the card, and one angle was slightly out, you would find that the shapes buckled and the card would not lie flat.

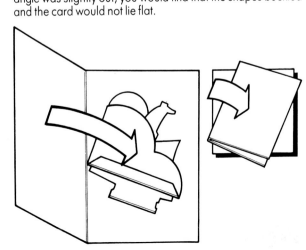

chapter three

FOLDING CARTONS

Folding cartons are containers made from sheets of board which have been cut, creased and scored for bending into desired shapes. This section introduces some of the most common constructions. Modifications to these are limited only by the ingenuity of the designer.

The rapid growth of self-service retailing has created a huge demand for packaging that not only carries and protects the product but also provides sales appeal. Folding cartons satisfy these criteria exceptionally well; infinitely variable in size, shape and design, and suited to high-quality graphic reproduction, they can be used to motivate the consumer to purchase one particular brand in preference to another. In addition they are economical to produce and assemble and, being collapsible, take up minimum space in storage and transit (the cartons are shipped and stored flat, and erected at the point at which they are to be filled).

When designing a folding carton for a particular product, bear in mind that it must be strong enough to protect the product and attractive enough to sell it. It must also be capable of being assembled, filled and closed quickly by hand or machine, and have suitable opening, reclosing and dispensing features for consumer use. The board you choose must be strong, yet light enough to be economical, pliable enough to fold and crease without cracking, and have a suitable surface for printing.

Folding boxboard, and duplex board (see page 15) are suitably pliable and resilient. Depending on the volume of the carton and the weight of the contents, choose a board from ·014 inch/ 350 microns up to ·025 inch/640 microns thick. Anything thinner than this will not be stiff enough for the purpose, and anything thicker will not crease properly.

Folding cartons fall into three broad categories: tube (end-load), tray (top load) and special construction.

Tube or shell cartons are one-piece constructions whose ends may be glued, tucked or locked. The bottom flaps may have special locking tabs to prevent heavy objects from sliding out. They are commonly used for packaging pourable solid products, eg detergents and dry mixes, and cosmetics and pharmaceuticals.

Tray or top-load cartons can be either one-piece or two-piece constructions. These are used for packaging multiple products, confectionery and fast foods, and may be fitted with an inset tray for the display of gift items.

Special constructions Cartons that do not fit either tube or tray descriptions, such as bottle-carrier cartons, blister packages, and so on.

TUCK-IN END CARTON
This design is for a standard carton with tuck-in lid and base, suitable for holding tubes, bottles and small objects. The carton is made from a single piece of card, with one gluing, and can be made to any dimensions you like.
Example illustrated measures 5in/127mm x 3¹/₂in/90mm x 2¹/₄in/57mm.

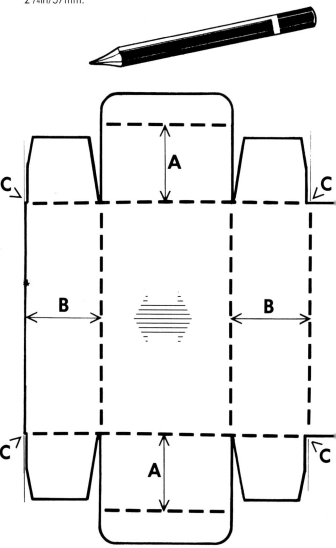

1. Draw up plan of carton to required dimensions. Card grain runs widthways. Dimensions **A** are ¹/₂mm shorter than dimensions **B**, to facilitate easy insertion of flap on lid when closing. Outer edges of corner flaps **C** are stepped back by ¹/₂mm to allow room for tuck-in flap on lid.

2. Cut out and crease along all dotted lines. Pre-bend all creases. Apply glue or double-sided tape to underside of glue flap. Remove backing strip from tape and bring up sides to form up carton, taking care to line up glue flap with edge of carton accurately. Push carton flat and apply pressure along glue area to secure.

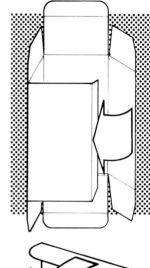

*See inside front and rear cover for key

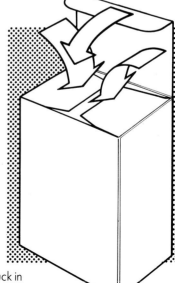

3. Form up carton and tuck in panels at top and base as shown.

CRASH-LOCK CARTON BASE

This is designed to take a heavier weight than the normal tuck-in carton base. As with the auto-lock base (see page 58) the base panels are tucked in and braced against each other to give added strength and reduce the risk of the base opening out accidentally. Example illustrated measures 5in/127mm × 3½in/90mm × 2¼in/57mm.

*See inside front and rear cover for key

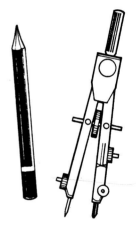

1. Draw up plan of carton body and lid to required dimensions, and draw up base as in diagram. Card grain runs widthways.

- Dimensions **A** must equal half dimensions **B**.
- Dimensions **C** are equal, and must be no longer than half of dimensions **D**.
- All dimensions marked **E** must be equal and the same as **F**.
- Corners marked **G** align with centre of dimensions **B**.

2. Cut out carton, crease along all dotted lines and pre-bend creases. Assemble carton by bringing front panel over and gluing in place using double-sided tape. To close base of box, fold in panels in sequence shown.

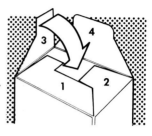

3. Gently push in panel 4 until it locates through slot.

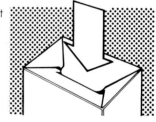

4. The base panels should join up neatly.

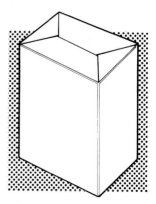

AUTO-LOCK CARTON BASE

This design makes a very strong, secure base, suitable for cartons holding heavy or breakable objects. It is also easy to erect once assembled: the base panels automatically lock together as the carton is formed up.

Carton illustrated measures 5¼in/140mm × 5in/127mm × 2¼in/64mm.

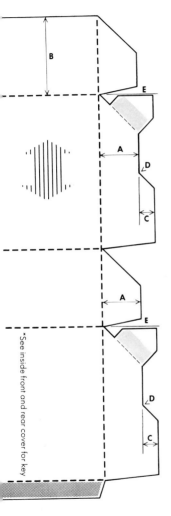

1. Draw up plan of carton to dimensions required, following the diagram. Card grain runs widthways.

*See inside front and rear cover for key

- Dimensions **A** are equal to half dimensions **B**, so that flaps meet exactly in centre when carton is assembled.
- Dimensions **C** should be not less than 15mm, even deeper if making a larger carton. This ensures a strong grip when base panels are locked together.

● Points **D** should align exactly with centre of front and back of carton so that they meet at the centre when carton is assembled.
● All diagonals on diagram must be exactly 45° to ensure a tight fit when carton is assembled.
● Edges of glue flaps **E** are set back from vertical crease line by 3mm.

2. Cut out carton and crease along all dotted lines. Perforate lines indicated on glue flaps with 3mm cuts. Avoid cutting too close to outer edges to reduce risk of tearing. Pre-bend all creases and pre-bend perforations in opposite

direction. Open out all panels. Apply double-sided tape to upper side of glue flap on side of carton and reverse side of glue flaps on base. Remove backing strip from tape on side of carton only and assemble carton by folding front over. Press carton flat to secure tape in place.

3. Turn carton on its side and, with base facing you, push all base panels right inside carton, making sure that glue flaps are facing outwards, as in diagram. Peel off backing strip from tape on glue flaps.

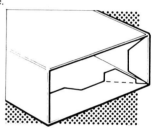

4. Gently push carton flat: push towards the left – not the right. Apply pressure to glue areas.

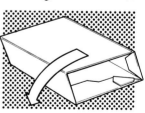

5. Base panels will automatically lock as carton is erected.

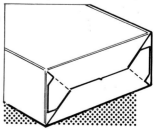

POP-UP CARTON LID
The carton lid design given on page 54 is fine for most purposes, but in certain cases the design illustrated below has a number of advantages. First, it is stronger. Second, it gives a more professional finish because there are no raw edges on view — a point worth considering if the carton is to be printed in a dark colour, as the white raw edges would then be noticeable. Third, the lid pops up automatically when opened, allowing the contents of the carton to be quickly and easily removed.
Example illustrated measures 5in/127mm x 3¹/₂in/90mm x 2¹/₄in/57mm.

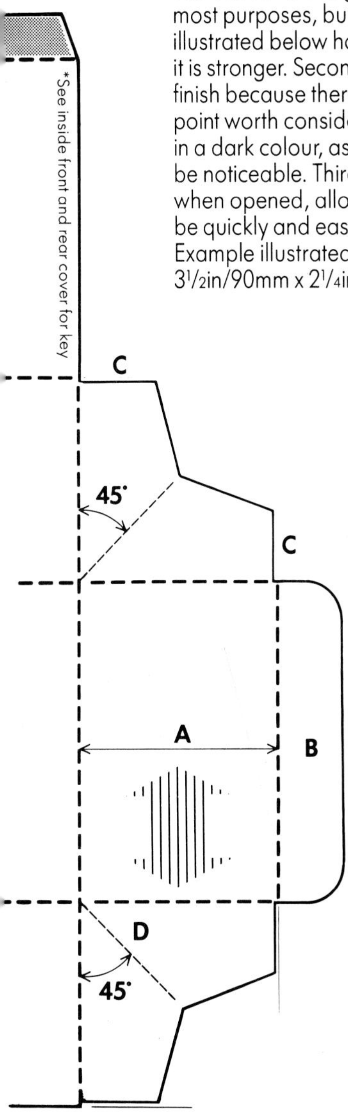

*See inside front and rear cover for key

C

45°

C

A

B

D

45°

1. Draw up plan of carton body and base to required dimensions. Draw plan of lid as in diagram. Card grain runs widthways.

● Start by drawing centre panel **A**, whose front-to-back dimension should be 1mm shorter than the width of side of carton: this allows room for tuck-in flap **B** on lid to be inserted into carton when closing.

● Tuck-in flap **B** should be no less than 15mm deep, otherwise it may slip out of carton. For larger cartons, it should be even deeper.

● Note shape of ends of tuck-in flap. The corners are rounded, but the sides are straight. This gives the flap a better grip on the inside of the carton when lid is closed: if the corners are too rounded the lid may pop open.
● Edges marked **C** on side panels are set back by 1mm to allow room for insertion of tuck-in flap on lid when closing.
● Make sure that perforation lines **D** on side flaps are angled at exactly 45°.

Cut out carton and crease along all dotted lines. Using the tip of a scalpel, perforate lines marked **D** with 4mm cuts. Start first cut at base and work upwards, ensuring that last cut is not too close to outer corner, otherwise corner will be weakened and liable to tearing.

2. Pre-bend all creases and perforations and assemble carton by bringing front panel over and gluing in place.

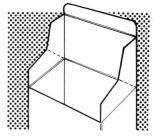

3. Close lid by pushing down. As lid is closed, side panels automatically bend inwards along perforated lines. As lid is opened, side panels spring open.

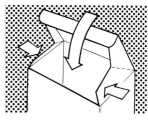

4. Completed lid in closed position.

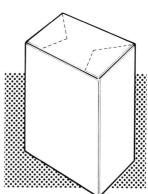

PILLOW PACK

A simple but effective design for a pillow-shaped novelty carton
with curved ends, suitable for holding small gift items such as
jewellery, bottles of perfume, etc. The pack is made from a single
piece of card and has one gluing.
Example illustrated measures 5in/127mm x 4in/101mm x 1in/25mm

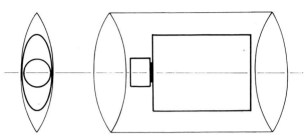

1. Start by measuring up the dimensions of the object to be
carried in the carton, ie height, width and depth at widest point.
The depth is particularly important, since this will determine the
shape and dimensions of the elliptical ends of the pack. Say the
object is a bottle: measure its circumference at the widest point
and, on a sheet of paper, draw a circle. Draw a line through the
centre of the circle, then draw freehand arcs around the circle to
get an idea of the width and depth required for the pack. The
arcs should fit snugly over the object at the widest point and
curve away gently; the angle of curve should not be too steep,
otherwise the pack will not work.

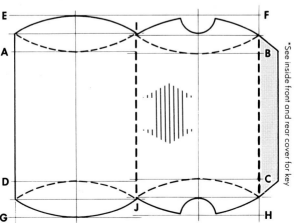

*See inside front and rear cover for key

2. Having established dimensions of pack, draw up a plan on a
sheet of card, as in diagram. Card grain runs lengthways. Start

with rectangle **ABCD**, drawn lightly, to height of object and
twice width of arcs drawn in your sketch. Then draw lines **EF**
and **GH** to form top and base of carton, whose depth is equal
to depth of object. Draw light pencil lines through centres of top
and base, horizontally and vertically; these form the major and
minor axes for drawing the elliptical ends of the carton. Draw
centre crease line **IJ**.

With compass point anywhere along vertical centre lines, draw
arcs forming panels for top and base of carton (use trial and
error until you find correct radius). Ellipses on right-hand side
must be stepped back 1mm, so that left-hand panels can be
folded over right-hand panels when closing carton.

Draw 'thumbnail' indents centred along top edges of right-hand
panels. These should be no deeper than half depth of panel.
Draw glue flap down right-hand side of carton, approximately
13mm wide.

3. Cut out and crease along all dotted lines. Work carefully
when creasing the curved ends: keep the creasing stick
going straight along the creasing rule while turning the
card in a clockwise direction (see page 11). Pre-bend all
creases. Apply double-sided tape to underside of glue flap.
Fold glue flap in, remove backing strip, fold carton over along
centre crease and apply pressure along glue area.

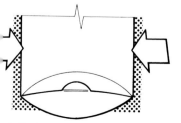
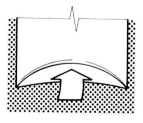

4. To close carton, press inwards along edges, then fold top
and base panels in over each other.

DOUBLE-WALLED CARTON

This is a very strong double-walled box with fold-in corners and tuck-in lid, made from a single piece of card with no gluings. It is easy to assemble and versatile in use: with the inclusion of a shaped inner tray (see page 66) it makes an attractive presentation box.

Example illustrated measures 7½in/190mm x 6in/152mm x 1½in/38mm.

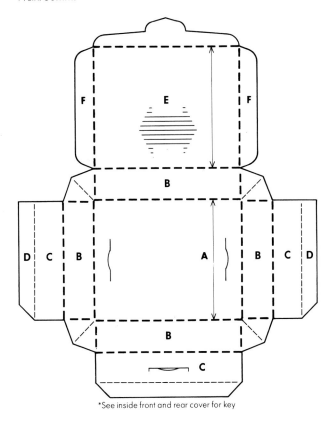

*See inside front and rear cover for key

1. Determine required dimensions of box. Draw up plan as in diagram.

- Outer walls **B** are 1mm aeeper than inner walls **C**, and ½mm longer at top and bottom. This allows clearance at front and back of box when outer walls are folded over inner walls.
- Locking flaps **D** should be 19mm deep and the front corners are angled at exactly 45°.

● Lid **E** is 1mm deeper than base **A** and 2mm narrower.
● Crease lines **F** on lid are set back by 1mm.

2. When carton is assembled, the fold-in corners are tucked in between the inner and outer walls, and tend to cause unsightly ridges if they come too high up the sides. To ensure that they don't, draw them as follows: Draw line **GH** at 45°, length equal to depth of wall **B**. Then connect points **HI** and **HJ**. Round off corners at **J** and **I**: this prevents a build-up of card at corners when folding walls over.

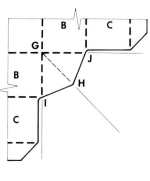

3. Cut out, crease and perforate where indicated on plan. Pre-bend all creases and perforation lines. To establish position of locking slots in base, lift front and rear walls and one side wall, tucking in corners as shown. Wrap inner wall **C** over so that locking flap lies flush with base of carton. Hold in this position and draw a line on base along edge of locking flap. Repeat for other side. Open out carton. Cut slits, centred on pencil lines, a third of depth of base in length. Slits should curve very slightly in the centre, curves facing outwards.

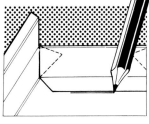

4. Erect carton again and lock base flaps into slits by pushing down at centre with thumbnail while pushing up from below with middle finger.

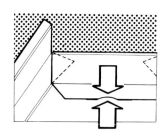

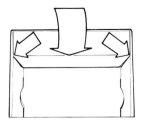

5. Fold in front wall. Close lid by slipping side flaps inside box but leaving front flap outside. Cut locking slot in front wall of carton following instructions given on page 35 (concertina booklet, step 6). Assemble box once again and close by inserting tongue on lid into slot on front wall.

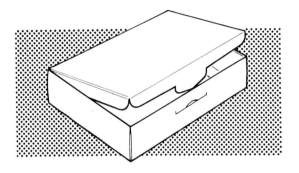

Optional inset tray

If the carton is intended for use as a gift or presentation box, an inset tray with shaped apertures for holding the gifts can be made as follows:

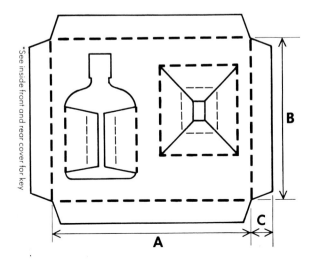

*See inside front and rear cover for key

1. Measure maximum depth of items to be displayed (this will determine depth of box). Draw up plan of tray as in diagram. **A** = width of base of box, minus 3mm to allow for double walls of carton being folded in. **B** = depth of box base, minus 2mm. **C** = half depth of box. When drawing the shaped apertures, make them 1mm larger all round than the items to be inserted. Cut out tray and make apertures as follows:

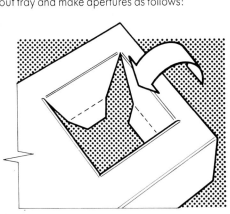

2. For square and rectangular apertures, cut, crease and perforate as indicated. Pre-bend creases. Pre-bend perforation in opposite direction to form flaps that fold back under display item to support it.

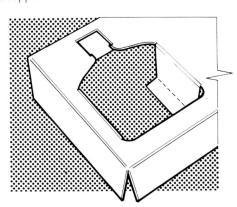

3. For rounded shapes such as bottles, cut along base and crease sides up to shoulders. Cut down centre and around neck and shoulders. If sides of bottle are not straight, it is easier simply to cut out aperture to shape of bottle (this also applies t

chapter four

PRESENTATION AND DISPLAY

The bulk of a card engineer's work involves designing point-of-sale price and promotional material for retail groups. This section covers display units, showcards and dispensers.

Display and promotional work offers the card engineer plenty of scope for creativity — and plenty of challenges too. When planning the design of a display stand, showcard or dispenser, you have to perform a juggling act between creating something which has maximum visual impact, is cost-effective, and which is easily assembled by the end user (what looks simple to you may look like a monkey's puzzle to a non-expert).

Cost-effectiveness is particularly important in this highly competitive field. Since paper and board represent 30%-50% of the cost of a finished job, it is important to ensure that your design can be printed and cut economically from a standard board size: an experienced card engineer may be able to interlock the shapes on the cutter diagram so that two blanks can be cut from one piece. Another costly part of the process is gluing, because it is labour intensive: this is why many showcards and dispensers are ingeniously constructed from a single sheet and have built-in support struts rather than separate ones which need to be glued on to the back.

No two jobs are ever the same, and each one comes with its own set of problems, not least of which is an often inadequate brief from the client. When picking up a brief, time spent asking questions is never wasted; it will save you a good deal of time and frustration later on when the client says "I like it, but I wanted it much bigger". The following checklist will help clarify the brief for any given design job.

What is the budget? (Is this a prestige job or a cheap one?)

Has client any design suggestions? (Is there a current advertising campaign to tie in with?)

What is the printed quantity? (10 off or 20,000? Keep quotes to a minimum)

How long must the item last in situ? (A hanging sign might last a year but a floor bin only a week)

Where is the display going? (Floor, counter, window, wall, door, ceiling?)

Who will erect the display? (Shop assistant, salesman or display team?)

Is the folded size important? (Will it go in a salesman's car?)

Is the item intended to hold product? (What is maximum weight? Ask for samples — full quantity if possible)

Are there any size restrictions? (Some stores allocate certain shelf areas.)

BOOK DISPLAY STAND

A one-piece, non-glued display stand suitable for holding flat, shallow items such as books, decorative plates, cartons, etc. The stand is very easy to erect and can be folded flat for storage.

Example illustrated measures 10½in/267mm x 7in/178mm. Platform width is 1¼in/30mm.

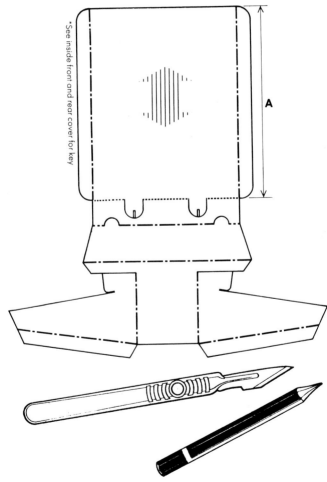

*See inside front and rear cover for key

1. Scale up diagram to required dimensions. If making to size above, dimension **A** is 9in/229mm. Cut out and score along lines indicated. Break all scores.

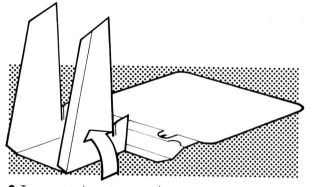

2. To erect stand, turn it over and raise up supporting struts as shown.

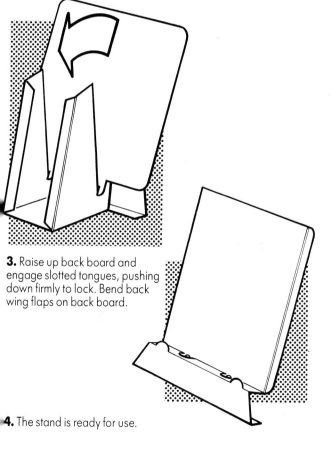

3. Raise up back board and engage slotted tongues, pushing down firmly to lock. Bend back wing flaps on back board.

4. The stand is ready for use.

DISPLAY STAND
A display stand with raised octagonal base, cut from two pieces
and with two gluings.
Example illustrated measures 18in/457mm across.

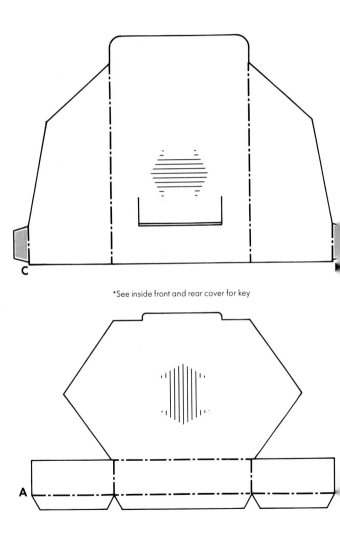

*See inside front and rear cover for key

1. Scale up diagram to size required. Cut out and score along
lines indicated. Break all scores.

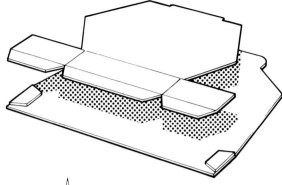

2. Apply glue or double-sided tape to undersides of glue flaps on back section. Fold glue flaps in and remove backing strips from tape. Lay base section on top of back section, lining up score line **AB** with base line **CD**. Apply pressure along glue area.

3. Stand unit up and push down platform section in base until tongue locates in slot in back section. Fold the three base flaps under. The display stand is now ready for use.

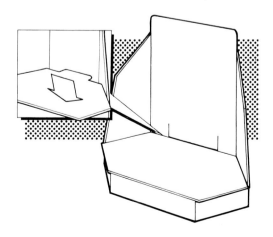

JUMBLE DISPENSER

This is a counter-top jumble dispenser with deep recess and
curved back, suitable for storing and displaying small items.
It is made from a single sheet of folding boxboard and has two
gluings. The advantage of this design is that it can be folded to a
small, convenient shape for storage or transit.
Example illustrated measures 12in/305mm x 11in/279mm x
8in/203mm.

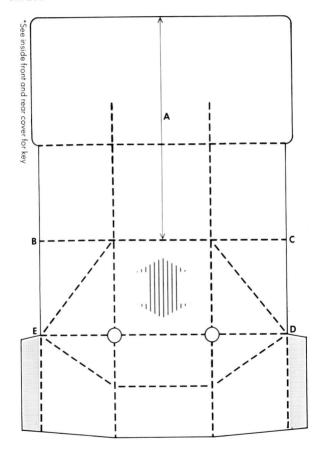

1. Scale up diagram to required dimensions. If making model to
size given above, dimension **A** is 12in/305mm. Cut and crease
along lines indicated, and pre-bend all creases.

2. Turn model over and fold bottom half up along line **BC**, then fold back again along line **DE**. Turn over again and apply glue or double-sided tape to glue flaps and stick down along edges.

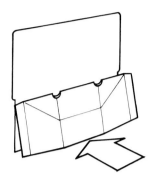

3. Turn model over once again and erect dispenser by gripping edges of base section in both hands and pushing inwards at edges while at the same time pressing downwards with thumbs along top edge of base. As you do this, the front tray opens out to form a deep, sloping recess.

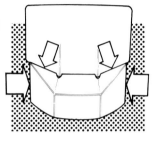

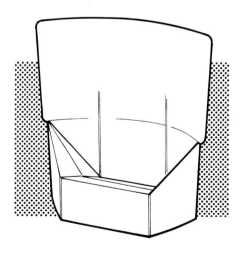

4. The completed model.

3-D SHOWCARD
This showcard incorporates a sloping base onto which samples of the product can be attached. The model is cut from a single piece of display board, with no gluings, and can be folded flat for storage and transit.
Example illustrated measures: 10½in/267mm (back) x 7¾in/197mm (base) when assembled.

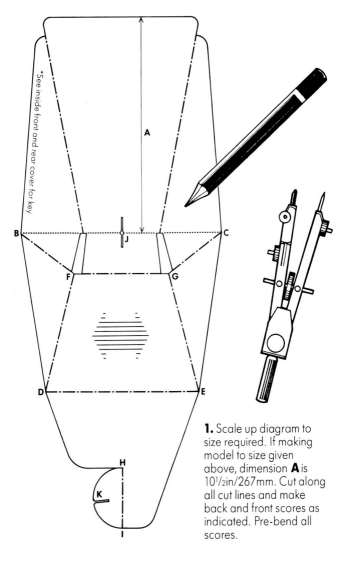

1. Scale up diagram to size required. If making model to size given above, dimension **A** is 10½in/267mm. Cut along all cut lines and make back and front scores as indicated. Pre-bend all scores.

2. To erect the showcard, fold up along crease **BC** until flat, then fold back along crease **DE**.

3. Fold base section down along crease **FG**, at the same time easing the two side wings backwards.

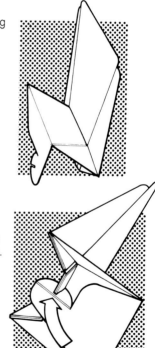

4. Fold bottom section back along crease **DE**, then fold in along score **HI** and engage the two slots **J** and **K** until they lock. (Diagram shows view from underneath.)

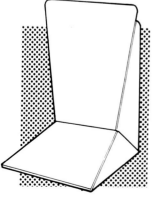

LEAFLET DISPENSER

This is the most commonly used type of leaflet dispenser. Cut from one piece of board, and with no gluings, it is economical to produce and easy to assemble. If the dispenser is to be printed, bear in mind that, when assembled, the print will appear on the reverse side of the back board – not the facing side.

Example illustrated measures 8in/203mm × 5¹/₂in/140mm when erected.

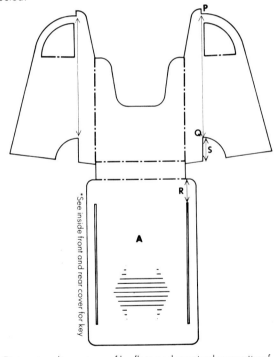

*See inside front and rear cover for key

1. Determine dimensions of leaflets and required capacity of dispenser and draw up plan as in diagram, constructing template for side supports as shown in steps 2 and 3. Height of back board **A** is 6mm shorter than height of leaflets.

2. The side supports require careful measuring so that they fit exactly into slots in back board when erected. The easiest way to proceed is to draw up one support on a piece of thin card and use this as a template when adding side supports to plan.

Start with vertical line **AB**, 20mm shorter than back board **A**. Draw base line **AC**, at least 101mm long and angled upwards at 7° from the horizontal. Draw line **DE** parallel to **AB**. Distance from **AB** is equal to required depth of leaflet holder. Draw line **FG**, distance from **DE** equal to thickness of board. Determine height of front of leaflet holder and plot this point (**H**) on line **AB**. Join **E** to **H** with a curved line, as in diagram, to form shoulder of leaflet holder.

3. On line **DE** mark point **I**, opposite **H**. Set compasses to radius **IE**, minus 6mm, and scribe an arc to **J** from line **DE**. Close compasses up 6mm. With centre **K**, scribe an arc from line **FG** to **L**. Draw line connecting **K** to **L**. Set compasses to radius 30mm. With centre **D**, scribe an arc **MN**. Mark point **O** 89mm from **D** on base line. Draw line connecting **O** to **J**.

4. Cut out template and place in position on diagram. Draw round template, turn over and place in position on opposite side. Note that corner **A** sits just below score line at base of leaflet holder – an amount equal to thickness of board.
Slots in back board equal length **PQ** on side support and inside edges align with score lines on front of holder. Width of slots is a fraction more than thickness of board. **R** equals **S**, minus thickness of board.

5. Cut out and score as indicated. Break all scores and assemble dispenser in sequence shown.

LEAFLET DISPENSER

This is a one-piece, non-glued leaflet dispenser with integral display panel, suitable for information, publicity or advertising purposes. In use, the dispenser is sturdy and well balanced, supported by a lock rudder strut at the back. It can be folded flat for storage.

Example illustrated measures 9³/₄in/248mm x 7¹/₂in/190mm.
· Leaflet holder section is 1³/₄in/44mm deep.

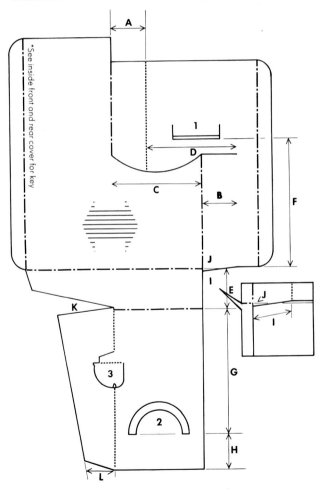

1. Before drawing up the plan, work out the dimensions required, based on the following measurements: dimension of leaflets to be held in holder, how much of leaflet area is to be

exposed above top of holder, how many leaflets are to be held, and how much display area is required adjacent to the leaflet holder section.

Having worked out the required height, width and depth of the model, draw up plan, bearing in mind the following points:

- **A** equals **B**. **C** equals **D**. **E** equals **A**.
- Slot **1** should be positioned no less than 15mm from top of panel **B**, and is centred across dimension **D**. Length of slot is equal to half of dimension **D**, and it should be no less than 3mm deep.
- Dimension **F** equals dimension **G**, which gives you position for base line of semi-circular locking device **2**, which is centred in panel. At this position, draw a line the same length as slot **1**. With compass point at centre of this line and pencil point at one end, scribe a semi-circle. Open compasses out to 6mm and scribe a second semi-circle.
- Dimension **H** should not be less than 40mm.
- Note that base line **I** (see detail) is cut on a slope of 3° from the horizontal so that when assembled the dispenser leans back very slightly: this helps to keep the leaflets upright and prevents them flopping forward. Inner corner **J** is dropped down below base line to a depth equal to the thickness of the board being used.
- Angle of edge **K** is exactly equal to angle of edge **I** and a minimum length of 65mm.
- Dimension **L** should be a minimum of 30mm.
- Draw locking mechanism **3** following instructions given on page 84.

2. Cut along all cut lines. Score and pre-bend all score lines. Make upward cuts 20mm long at each end of slot **1**. To assemble dispenser, turn over and form up leaflet holder section by pushing to the right.

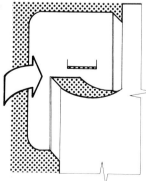

3. Lift up back support section and lock by inserting semi-circular tongue into slot and pushing it down.

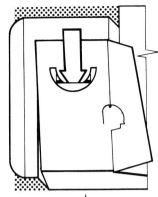

4. Open out support strut and lock in position by pushing down locking mechanism. Fold back side returns.

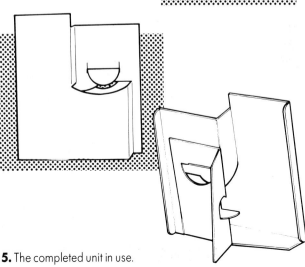

5. The completed unit in use.

SUPPORTING STRUTS

If possible, it is preferable to build a back support into the overall design of display units and showcards, avoiding the necessity for a separate strut that has to be glued on to the back, thus adding to the production costs. However, this is not always feasible, and large floorstanding displays in particular may require a separate supporting strut to keep them upright. Since the grain of the board runs widthways on most showcards, a strut will also provide a vertical brace which prevents the showcard from warping.

Small-to-medium sized struts are usually made from display board, between ·050 inch/1250 microns and .080 inch/2000 microns in weight. For larger struts, corrugated board is more economical. To give maximum support, the strut should extend almost to the top of the showcard. When making up a prototype, ensure that the strut is glued on absolutely straight and that its bottom edge does not overlap the base of the showcard, otherwise the structure becomes unstable. For easier and more accurate positioning, glue the strut in place in the flat, rather than setting it up and then positioning it.

There are several different types of strut, suitable for different applications. Those in common use are:

Standard lock rudder strut Suitable for showcards up to approximately 356mm/14in high × 305mm/12in wide.

Box strut Stronger and more stable than the lock rudder strut. Will support showcards up to approximately 762mm/30in high.

Easel strut A durable construction suitable for use with showcards that are likely to be moved around frequently in use. Provides a lot of support at the base.

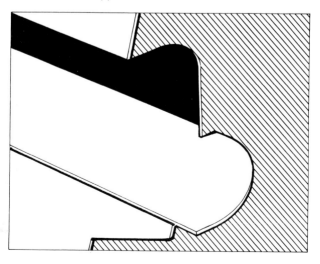

LOCK RUDDER STRUT

This is the standard lock rudder strut, commonly used for supporting small- to medium-sized showcards.
Example illustrated measures 10in/254mm high.

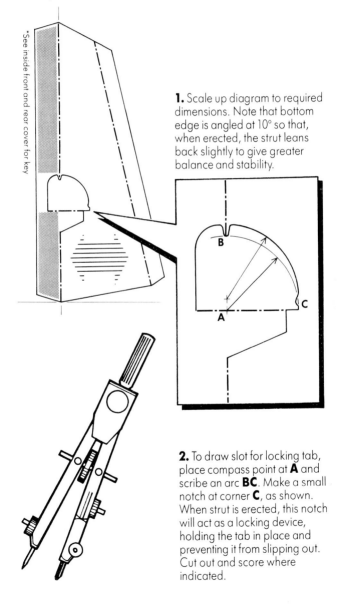

*See inside front and rear cover for key

1. Scale up diagram to required dimensions. Note that bottom edge is angled at 10° so that, when erected, the strut leans back slightly to give greater balance and stability.

2. To draw slot for locking tab, place compass point at **A** and scribe an arc **BC**. Make a small notch at corner **C**, as shown. When strut is erected, this notch will act as a locking device, holding the tab in place and preventing it from slipping out. Cut out and score where indicated.

3. Draw a vertical line down exact centre of back of showcard. Apply glue along flap and stick to centre of showcard. Ensure base of strut does not overhang base of showcard. To erect strut, open out and bring down locking tab as shown, squeezing it past notch in side until it locks in place.

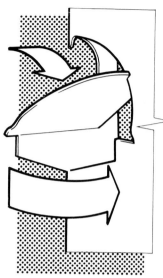

4. The finished strut in place.

5. This variation of the lock rudder strut includes an extra piece at the top with a small hole punched in it, for use with showcards that are to be hung from the wall.

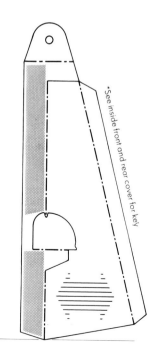

*See inside front and rear cover for key

DOUBLE LOCK RUDDER STRUT

This design basically comprises
two lock rudder struts joined
together and gives extra
support to very large,
heavy showcards.
Example illustrated
is 20 in/508 mm high.

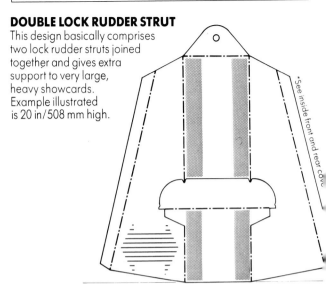

*See inside front and rear cover

1. Scale up diagram to required dimensions. Cut out and score
where indicated, and break scores.

2. Draw locating lines on back
of showcard to width of glue
area, at 90° to the bottom
edge. Apply glue to reverse side
of glue area. Turn the strut
over, lay it flat and glue it down
centre of showcard, lining up
edges of glue area with locating
lines on showcard. Hold locking
device down and fold the side
sections back. Pull down locking
device until it locks in place.

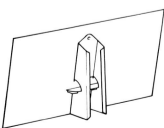

3. The finished strut in place.

EASEL STRUT

The easel strut is used where a showcard requires plenty of stability at the base, for example if it is narrower at the base than at the top. It is economical to produce as it uses up less board than, for example, a box strut. Example illustrated is for use with an A4 showcard.

1. Scale up diagram to 13in/330mm high (for an A4 size showcard).

2. Cut out and score. Break all scores. Apply glue to outer edges of panel **A** on the upper side. Draw a horizontal line to length of line **BC** 40mm up from base of showcard and centred across the back. Turn strut over and remove backing strip from tape. Lay strut on top of showcard as shown, with score line **BC** butting up to pencil line. Apply pressure along glue areas.

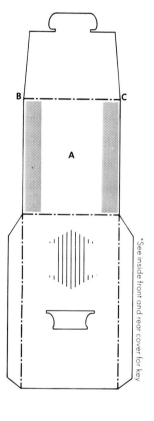

*See inside front and rear cover for key

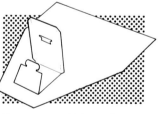

To erect strut, lift lower flap and bring down upper flap. Insert tongue through slot. To lock, pull tongue forward till it engages.

3. The completed strut in position.

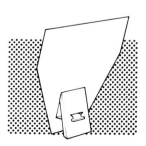

BOX STRUT

This is a very sturdy strut with feet, used for very large, wide showcards. It is relatively expensive to produce commercially, as it involves two gluings.

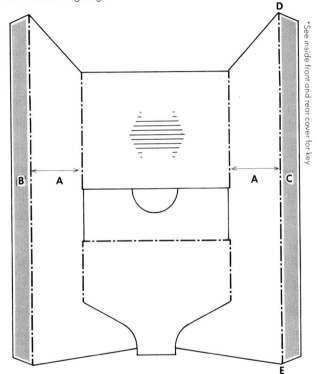

*See inside front and rear cover for key

1. Scale up diagram to required dimensions. As a guide, if the strut is to be up to 3ft/914mm high, dimensions **A** should be about 3½in/89mm wide. If it is up to 6ft/1829mm high, dimensions **A** should be about 5in/127mm wide. Make the centre panels as wide as possible.
2. Cut out and score. Break all scores. Apply glue or double-sided tape to glue flaps. Draw two locating lines on back of showcard to width of centre panel, making sure they are accurately centred across the back. Remove backing strip from glue flap **B.** Line up score line **DE** with left pencil line (line it up at the bottom edge first to make sure it doesn't hang below base of showcard) and glue down. Remove tape from glue flap **B** and fold in. Bring body of strut over and glue down, again checking that bottom of strut does not hang below base of showcard.

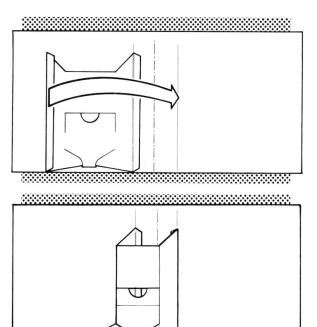

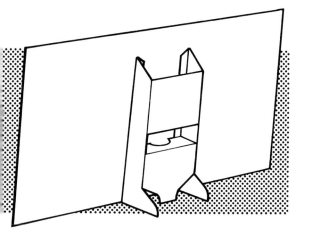

3. To erect, open out strut and lock by pushing centre flap down.

SELF-LOCKING DROP STRUT

It is possible to give a three-dimensional look to a showcard or display stand by attaching additional cut-out shapes or panels to the main piece. The cut-out shape is attached by means of a self-locking drop strut, which holds it proud of the main piece.

1. Start by drawing a side elevation of the showcard to scale. Dimensions **A** are determined by the required amount of space between the main showcard and the additional panel. Dimension **B** should be slightly shorter than the panel to which it is attached, so that it doesn't show. Dimension **C** is determined by dimensions **A** and **B**. (This piece is the locking section, which braces the strut and prevents it from sagging.) Dimensions **D** are glue flaps.

2. Having worked out the dimensions of the strut, draw up plan as in diagram on a piece of display board. Cut out and make front scores where indicated. Break all scores.

3. Turn strut over and glue section B to back of panel, positioning it centrally. Fold strut up along line **EF** and then fold down along line **GH**, so that section **C** is underneath.

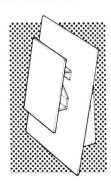

4. Turn over and glue in position on front of main display (first measure depth of section **A** and glue the panel higher up than required, to this dimension; when the strut is erected, the panel drops down by this amount.)

FRICTION STRUT

This is not a support strut, but a girdering piece; it is used with showcards that are particularly long, either vertically or horizontally, and helps to prevent warping and bending of the card. A series of slots and tongues is made along the centre of the strut to form a 'hinge'; one half of the strut is glued to the back of the showcard and the other is hinged back to provide a brace.

1. Determine required length of strut and draw up plan as in diagram. All slots and tongues should be of equal length. As a guide, make them about 1in/25mm long for a strut 12in/305mm long; for a strut 24in/610mm long, make the slots and tongues each 2in/51mm long.

2. Cut out strut and cut and score where indicated on diagram in step 1. When cutting the 'teeth', ensure that they stand proud of the folded strut by 1/2mm. To measure this accurately, take a spare piece of board, score it, measure the depth of the score and add 1/2mm to that measurement.

3. Apply glue to one half of the strut and glue in position on back of showcard, with the non-glued half uppermost. It is important that the strut is glued on the flat and then folded back, to ensure the teeth get a firm grip.

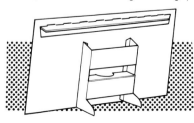

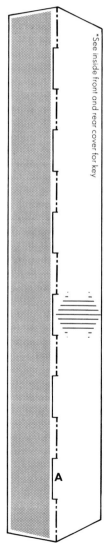

*See inside front and rear cover for key

A

ACKNOWLEDGEMENTS

Series editor: Judy Martin
Text: Angela Gair
Art direction: Nigel Osborne
Design: Sally Stockwell
Artwork: Peter Serjeant and Peter Owen

AN OUTLINE PRESS BOOK

© IAN HONEYBONE 1990
First published in Great Britain in 1990 by
Outline Press (Book Publishers) Limited
115J Cleveland Street
London W1P 5PN

ISBN 1.871547.03.2

This book was designed and produced by
THE OUTLINE PRESS

Typesetting by Midford Typesetting Ltd.

Printed and bound by Grafoimpex, Zagreb, Yugoslavia.

00036884
736.98

736.98

LUTON SIXTH FORM COLLEGE

LIBREX